The Project Manageme

# Defining Project Work
# – Simplified!

Michael B Bender

*The Project Management Mini-Series*

**Defining Project Work - Simplified!**
Published: June, 2014

Published by: Ally Publishing Group, Sugar Grove, IL 60554
Defining Project Work - Simplified!
Please forward comments and suggestions to:
    AllyPublishingGroup@AllyBusiness.com

Michael B. Bender

"PMI", "PMP" and "PMBOK" are registered trademarks of the Project Management Institute, Newtown Square, PA.

"Microsoft Project" is a registered trademark of Microsoft Corporation.

Company and product names mentioned herein are the trademarks or registered trademarks of their respective owners.

ISBN-10: 1-940441-08-0
ISBN-13: 978-1-940441-08-5

# DEDICATION

To my brother David, who put up with all my issues and never gave up on me.

# PREFACE

## ABOUT THE SERIES

I specifically designed the Project Management Mini-Series for busy project managers. Project management is a vast topic. While no particular aspect of project management is difficult, mastering all the necessary skills to make a project successful just takes time.

You'll face many issues in your journey to master the discipline; some you'll handle nicely, but some will involve skills that may be new to you. You'll want professional-level answers to specific project management questions quickly. I designed the Project Management Mini-Series for just such occasions.

The books are short, inexpensive, written for professional project managers, and designed to be easy-to-read. They get to the point, demonstrate how to apply the skill, they offer tools and techniques and then allow you to get on your way.

The series is not just for new project managers. I include three levels of books, color-coding the levels for quick recognition:

- Simplified! (Hunter Green)  For new or novice project managers
- Skilled (Royal Blue) for novice to moderate skill levels
- Advanced (Gold) for more advanced techniques

Some key features I included in the books:

- Templates, forms, charts and checklists with descriptions on how to use them.

- You can download electronic copies of the templates, forms and other tools for project management on my company's web site: www.AllyBusiness.com/pm-tools. Adjust them for your own style and use them.

- Download specific forms, images and samples from books at www.AllyBusiness.com/dpw-simplified.

- "Tricks of the Trade" is a section I include in each book. This section offers specific techniques I and many of my colleagues use to accomplish the goals and tasks involved in the topic.

I hope you find the series useful. Please feel free to e-mail me with comments and suggestions at: PM-Mini-Series@AllyBusiness.com.

# ABOUT THE BOOK

I selected this topic as the second book in the series since defining the work is the heart of project management. Defining the work required to complete the project successfully is likely the single most important activity in project management. Certainly, you can't develop the work without clear objectives and requirements, or understanding your stakeholders; but get this wrong and your project will always be a challenge. Get it right and the rest of the project can fall into place very nicely.

In this book, we address simple, practical and easily-implemented steps to defining project work. Formally called the Work Breakdown Structure (WBS), the work becomes the core of the project. Once created, it drives all aspects of the project, from risk management, to quality definition, team definition, communication, procurement, and all other aspects.

In recent years, the WBS has become very sophisticated. Terms like: work packages, phases, schedule activities, planning packages and many others have very specific meaning in advanced WBS's. These are not our quest in this book. While I will introduce you to several of these terms, I will reserve thorough discussions for more advanced books. In this book, I hope to set a solid foundation and allow you develop a successful WBS for small and medium-sized projects and make your projects successful as quickly and easily as I can. We can address more experienced topics as your experience level increases.

I hope this book brings you success!.

***Good luck, and may all your projects be successful!***

# CONTENTS

# 1 GETTING STARTED

Defining project work is the heart and soul of project management. Formally called the *Work Breakdown Structure* (WBS), the work definition will drive who's on your team; it will drive your risk management; you'll use it to communicate with stakeholders; it will be the basis of your outsourcing and procurements; the list goes on. Get this right, and your project will flow; get it wrong and it's unlikely you'll ever get on top of your project.

WBS's can become very sophisticated. While such sophistication can be beneficial in larger and more complex projects, a simple approach does quite well in most situations. Do understand however, that if you progress in project management, you'll likely change the way you do WBSs. You should find this transition simple, so there's no need for concern at this early stage. I'll cover more on this topic later.

First, let's define our goal.

## Work Breakdown Structures

A Work Breakdown Structure (WBS) is a hierarchical decomposition of the work needed in a project. Essentially, we figure out everything we need to do at a high level. We then break each of those steps down into smaller, more manageable steps. We continue this process until the steps are small enough to accurately estimate.

While that definition may seem a bit tedious, you're already familiar with WBSs. More simply stated: a WBS is a list of tasks needed to do something. Directions to a friend's house is a WBS. A recipe is a WBS. A *To-Do* list is a WBS, as is a meeting agenda. A syllabus for a course contains a WBS.

When you're preparing a meal, the highest level of the WBS might be "Prepare the meal". The next level down will be each course (appetizers, main course, dessert). The next level down will be each dish in the course (fish, vegetables, starch, etc.) The next level down will be the steps needed to create each dish. Here's how this WBS might look to a project manager:

*Sample WBS for a Meal*

1. Prepare the meal
    1.1. Prepare appetizers
        1.1.1. Prepare cheese tray
        1.1.2. Prepare finger sandwiches
        1.1.3. Prepare appetizer beverages
    1.2. Prepare main course
        1.2.1. Prepare fish
        1.2.2. Prepare asparagus
        1.2.3. Prepare cuscus
        1.2.4. Prepare beverages
    1.3. Prepare dessert
        1.3.1. Prepare ice cream
        1.3.2. Prepare coffee
        1.3.3. Prepare cookies

I presented this sample WBS in outline format. This is one of the two most common formats used for presenting a WBS. The other is a hierarchical chart format, similar to an organization chart. Here's the same WBS in hierarchical chart format.

Figure 1: Sample WBS for Preparing a Meal

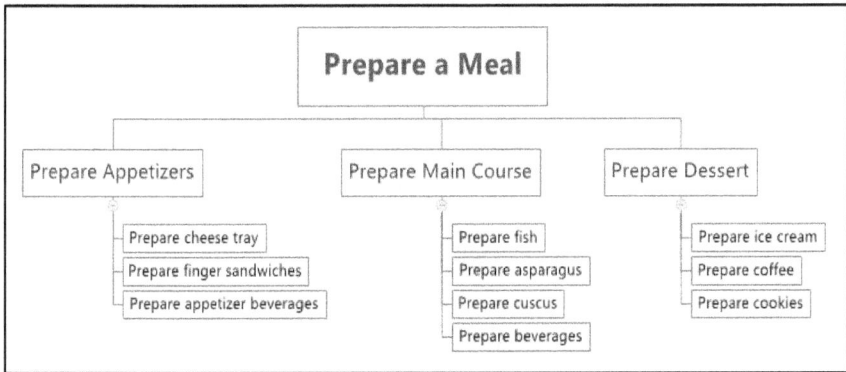

## Purpose of the WBS

The purpose of the WBS may seem obvious, however there are two important considerations that demands our attention. Formally, we derive a definition of the WBS from the Project Management Institute's (PMI's) *PMBOK® Guide*[1] page 105:

> ***The purpose of the WBS is to define ALL the work required and ONLY the work required to make the project successful.***

I highlighted the two considerations in all capitals. First, the WBS MUST contain ALL the work. I can't emphasize this enough. One of the most common mistakes both new and experienced project managers make is leaving out work elements from their WBS. Frequently this isn't because they didn't think of them. It's because they assume everyone knows you have to do them.

The second consideration is that the WBS should contain ONLY the work required for success. Too many project managers add work to projects absorbing money and resources but which don't add value and aren't needed for the project.

---

[1] Project Management Institute (2013). *The Guide to the Project Management Body of Knowledge (PMBOK® Guide)*, 5th edition. Newtown Square, PA.

This leads us to the two main rules for the WBS. When I build a WBS I just make sure there's:

- Nothing Missing
- Nothing Extra

Remember: the WBS should contain all the work required, and only the work required to make the project successful. Be thorough and DON'T ASSUME. What's intuitively obvious to you may not be to someone else. WRITE DOWN EVERY STEP.

Perhaps it is just as important to know what a WBS does not contain. When creating the WBS, we don't think about resources, the sequence of activities, costs, or any other aspects of the project. We only care about defining all the tasks. We just want the list of tasks: nothing more and nothing less (starting to notice a pattern?)

This discussion leads us nicely into a brief discussion of breakdown structures.

## Breakdown Structures

Our brief description of WBS's offers us the basic concepts of a breakdown structure in general. *Breakdown structures* are hierarchical decompositions of anything. In project management, there are several: the Work Breakdown Structure (WBS), the Resource Breakdown Structure (essentially, the team organization chart), the Goals Breakdown Structure (GBS, a hierarchical decomposition of project objectives), and several others. Many breakdown structures exist outside of project management. A Bill of Materials (BOM) is a breakdown structure. An ingredients list for a food dish is a breakdown structure. Look around and you'll find many more examples.

All breakdown structures have the same characteristics. They're a hierarchical decomposition. They exhibit the same two rules: nothing missing, nothing extra.

## Our Scope for this Book

This book presents simple and practical methods for developing a WBS. If you're new to project management, I encourage you to follow these steps as they will help you succeed quickly. As you progress in your development as a project manager, you'll discover that the characteristics of the WBS will change. Surprisingly, sophisticated WBS's don't actually contain any work at all. These are called "deliverables-oriented" WBS's and they actually contain only a list of deliverables and components of those deliverables. The key distinction is that in this book, the WBS contains actions (verbs) and the deliverables-oriented WBS contains items (nouns). You need not be concerned about this distinction at this point.

Also, in this book we don't concern ourselves with any other aspect of the project. We don't worry about resources, costs, requirements, deliverables, risks, etc., except that they offer us insight into our WBS. Our goal is simply define all the work needed for the project. Certainly, these other aspects help us define the WBS and I will address them as necessary, but I will leave detailed discussions of these aspects to other texts.

# 2 YOUR FIRST WORK PLAN

I find in my travels that many people have difficulty building their first WBS. The reason is that many of us were never taught how to think through a series of steps to achieve a goal. Think back to grade school. You were told what to do, when to do it, and how to do it. Rarely were you asked to devise your own strategy for getting something done.

When you're doing a project at home, how many times do you go back to Home Depot for items you missed or didn't consider? How much faster could you get that project done if you only went to Home Depot once?

So, if you find yourself struggling a bit the first time out, don't be too concerned. It's an easy skill to master, but it does take a bit of experience. So, let's begin.

## Initial Drivers

The WBS is not the first element we develop in the project plan. The proper (albeit simplified) sequence is: 1) develop the charter, 2) create the list of deliverables, 3) define the requirements, then 4) create the WBS. Of the three predecessors, the deliverables and requirements are the two key elements needed for defining the work. I will call these the *initial drivers*.

Certainly, the purpose of work is to produce a product or other result. In order to successfully define the work, we must first define the products and results. We do this by defining the deliverables and requirements.

**Deliverables** are the complete list of all the things we'll give the customer plus all the things we need to create internally. For simplicity, let's assume we're building a table for some specific purpose. Let's say we're building a table for a trade show for the marketing department. In this situation, the marketing department is our customer and the key deliverable is the table.

However, in order to create the table we'd have to design it, purchase materials (which will require a bill of materials) and test it. So, we'd need a design, a test plan and checklists, and a bill of materials. These are also deliverables, but as the customer won't see these. We call them *internal* deliverables. We need to produce them to create the table but the customer will never see them. The customer will get the table. To distinguish this deliverable, we'll call it a *customer* deliverable.

Make sure you include ALL the deliverables when building your work plan: both internal and customer deliverables. If you leave something out you'll forget to include the work needed to build it. Then you'll find yourself behind the project.

**Requirements** are most easily described as the characteristics of the deliverables needed for success. Using our table example, the table must have specific dimensions to fit inside the trade show booth. Marketing might also require electrical outlets in the table to power computers or other electronic displays that will sit on the table. Marketing might require shelving or drawers for storing brochures, electronic equipment, pens, etc.

These types of requirements are called *product* requirements as they describe the products or deliverables the customer will receive. While critical, product requirements alone are insufficient to define all the work in a project. We must also include *project* requirements. Project requirements may include such items as safety or compliance regulations. Additionally, the project manager must communicate with stakeholders, manage project risks, buy materials, hire contractors, etc.

These items also must be included in both the requirements and work breakdown structure. I will cover these areas more in chapter 4.

### Defining the High Levels

Selecting the styles for the upper levels of the WBS is a matter of choice. For small projects, the deliverables themselves will do nicely. If you do this, you're actually starting a *deliverables-oriented* WBS as described earlier. For medium or larger projects, most project manager use *phases* which are also based on deliverables. However, you can use any high-level composition you like. For example, if you're doing a national sales promotion project and you divide the nation into regions, you can use the regions for your upper levels. That way you can define the work to be performed in the Northeast Region, the Southeast Region, etc. See figure 2. You'll find other examples in the appendix.

Figure 2: Sample WBS for Regional Sales Promotion

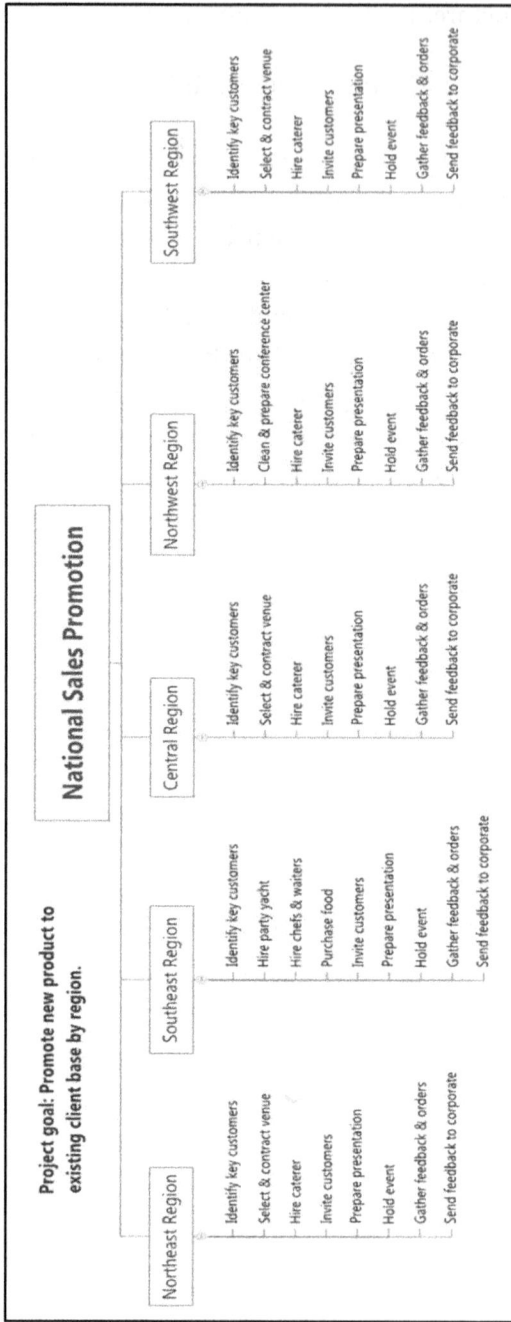

**Project goal: Promote new product to existing client base by region.**

**National Sales Promotion**

**Northeast Region**
- Identify key customers
- Select & contract venue
- Hire caterer
- Invite customers
- Prepare presentation
- Hold event
- Gather feedback & orders
- Send feedback to corporate

**Southeast Region**
- Identify key customers
- Hire party yacht
- Hire chefs & waiters
- Purchase food
- Invite customers
- Prepare presentation
- Hold event
- Gather feedback & orders
- Send feedback to corporate

**Central Region**
- Identify key customers
- Select & contract venue
- Hire caterer
- Invite customers
- Prepare presentation
- Hold event
- Gather feedback & orders
- Send feedback to corporate

**Northwest Region**
- Identify key customers
- Clean & prepare conference center
- Hire caterer
- Invite customers
- Prepare presentation
- Hold event
- Gather feedback & orders
- Send feedback to corporate

**Southwest Region**
- Identify key customers
- Select & contract venue
- Hire caterer
- Invite customers
- Prepare presentation
- Hold event
- Gather feedback & orders
- Send feedback to corporate

## Decomposition

Once you've defined the higher levels, the rest of the WBS becomes relatively easy. We simply decompose the higher level down into more detail. This is called *decomposition*. Just keep remembering the two rules: nothing missing, nothing extra. Make sure each decomposition is complete and you don't add anything extra into each decomposition.

The trick to making this work is to mentally put yourself in the situation then think through the steps in your mind. Questions I ask myself include:

- "What do I need to have in my hands to start this activity?"
- "If I do these [lower-level] activities, will I complete the next higher one?
- "Is there anything in this list I don't have to do to accomplish the higher layer?"

With experience you'll create your own list of questions. For now, let's use mine and look at an example. First, let's try a child's birthday party. Let's define the upper-layer work elements as: Preparation, The Party, and Cleanup. Let's start with Preparation.

**Preparation** is the first major step (or phase, if you like). So, I ask, "What do I need to have in my hands to start this activity?". Since this is the first step any answer to this question must be the deliverables and requirements.

One requirement is that the activities be age-appropriate. Other requirements for the party may include: safety, fun, inexpensive, comfortable and convenient for my child's friends' parents, etc. I establish a budget. I pick a date convenient for myself and my child's friend's parents: ideally on or close to my child's actual birthday.

NOTE: In practice you wouldn't write these down; they'll be in your head. But in a project plan I certainly would write them down. We started our first WBS:

1. Preparation
   1.1. Determine budget
   1.2. Select date
   1.3. Create list of friends
   1.4. Create a list of age-appropriate, fun and safe activities

Next question, "If I do these activities, will I have completed the upper level?" For this phase this translates to: "Will I be prepared for the party?" To do this, I mentally put myself in the morning of the party and image everything is going smoothly. That means I have a clear schedule of activities, I know who's showing up, I know the chaperones, I know how we're getting to and from the venue (if it's not at my house), I know the finances and have ensured a safe environment. You'll want to give the attendees a small gift bag, and you'll need to purchase some items for the party (cake, decorations, etc.) Let's now complete the first phase:

1. Preparation
   1.1. Determine budget
   1.2. Select date
   1.3. Create list of friends
   1.4. Create a list of age-appropriate, fun and safe activities
   1.5. Check activity list with child
   1.6. Create list of contacts
   1.7. Create and send invitations
   1.8. Receive invitation responses
   1.9. Select activities
   1.10. Schedule activities
   1.11. Vet suppliers
   1.12. Determine and confirm chaperones
   1.13. Determine and confirm transportation
   1.14. Select and purchase gift bags, decorations and party items
   1.15. Select and buy presents

Notice how it got bigger? Had I not put myself into the morning of the party I would have left a lot of items out. Now, again I ask, "If I do these activities, will I have completed the upper level?" In other words, "Am I all ready the morning of the party?" If the answer is "yes", then that phase is done and we can proceed to the next phase.

**This is important**: As you proceed to the next phase, you may discover something missing from the first. It's okay to go add it. It's only paper at this point. This is one of the benefits of planning. Having the ability to go back and fix earlier steps in paper is much less expensive and frustrating than having to do it for real. It's like going back to Home Depot because you forgot to buy something, then going back again, and again…

Note that for something as simple as a child's birthday party, we've listed 15 work elements just for the preparation phase. Also note that some elements are rather large (vetting the suppliers, determine and confirm chaperones, purchasing gift bag and party items, etc.). Don't be surprised if a project that initially seems simple ends up with dozens or even hundreds of activities. Now also remember: the reason the activity list is large is because we don't assume anything. WRITE DOWN EVERY ACTIVITY! While it may be intuitively obvious to you it may not be to the person who will do the work. Also, if you leave a work activity out you'll forget to estimate it for schedule and costing purposes, or simply just forget to do it. Just get used to projects with many activities.

So, let's proceed. First, let's take one of the larger elements of the Preparation phase and decompose it. Let's take 1.11 Vet Suppliers. For our example, let's assume you're going to hire some entertainment. For one of our daughter's parties, we had a wonderful lady who had rescued some exotic pets that she would bring to parties. This seemed both fun and educational for the children; but of course, my wife and I were concerned about safety both for the children as well as the animals. The vetting process was significant. To find and vet such people you might perform the following steps:

1.11. Vet Suppliers
- 1.11.1.  Ask neighbors and friends for recommendations
- 1.11.2.  Create short list of possible entertainers
- 1.11.3.  Receive and check references
- 1.11.4.  Obtain costs and agendas
- 1.11.5.  Conduct phone interviews
- 1.11.6.  Check references
- 1.11.7.  Select vendor

As you can see, it's quite easy to get a large number of activities, even for a simple project. The process worked well for us. The lady was excellent. Her animals were both fun and kid-friendly as well as educational and it ended up being a very memorable birthday for our daughter as well as for my wife and myself.

The next phase would be the party itself. We created most of the elements for this phase from steps 1.9 and 1.10 in the previous phase (select activities and schedule activities). There are others, however. To discover them, again, mentally put yourself in the morning of the party. So, let's proceed to the next phase: The Party.

2. The Party
- 2.1. Prepare the site
- 2.2. Decorate
- 2.3. Prepare food
- 2.4. Confirm funds in checking account
- 2.5. Prepare gift bags and presents
- 2.6. Reconfirm chaperones
- 2.7. Receive guests and chaperones
- 2.8. Deal with overly-excited child
- 2.9. Hold the party (see results of 1.9 and 1.10)

The final phase, of course, is clean-up. As you develop this phase, you might realize that selecting the right decorations and party items would help clean-up quite a bit. For example, if we buy inexpensive but colorful plastic table cloths and use plastic utensils and paper plates, we can simply wrap up the table cloth with all the used utensil and plates in it for easy clean-up. Since we're thinking things through first, and we really didn't buy anything yet, we can go back to phase 1's plan and make appropriate adjustments. That's the beauty of planning. I'll let you work out the final phase on your own.

We've now completed our first WBS. As you can see, writing down every step, thinking things through and putting yourself in the situation offers great benefits even for simple projects. Now, let's get back to business and look at more formal tools and techniques for developing professional WBS's.

# 3 TRICKS OF THE TRADE

This section offers tools and techniques for developing WBS's. In my experience, all these are useful. I haven't found any one of these to be better or worse than any other. Each has advantages and disadvantages. I generally employ several techniques depending on my team, the project, senior management, and the overall organizational culture. I also haven't found any of these to be difficult. Go ahead and try them out as the spirit moves you. The only important thing is the result: that we define all the work required and only the work required for project success. At the end of this chapter I'll show how I might combine several of these.

Here's the list:

- Brainstorming
- Expert Analysis
- Templates
- Mind-Mapping
- Facilitated Sessions

Before I begin with the list, I MUST emphasis the first trick of the trade.

## Trick of the Trade #1: Forget the Schedule

Ever since Microsoft published Microsoft Project®, project managers invariably start their WBS using the Gantt chart, assigning durations and sequencing their WBS as they create it. DON'T! This is a mistake.

Forget durations. Forget resources. Forget sequencing. Forget the Gantt chart. It's the wrong place to start. Use a word processor to create an outline WBS, use mind-mapping software to create the WBS, grab yourself a flip chart and hand-write the WBS, but please, stay away from the Gantt chart. It's the wrong focus. Remember: we're defining work. We're not scheduling, we're not sequencing. That will come later. For now, just define the work.

## Brainstorming

Brainstorming is a great way to get started with almost any WBS. Most project managers find it fun for both themselves and their teams. It allows the team to participate in the projects, thereby generating buy-in and commitment. It's a great team-building exercise. It produces decent results and a bit of enthusiasm. Here's how it works.

Gather your team or simply ask for help from a group of experts and have them brainstorm all the activities needed to do the project. You can do this formally or informally, it doesn't matter. If you go formally you'll get a huge list of activities which you can sort out. If you go informally your list will be considerably smaller. It will require less post-session work, but will likely leave things out. Here's how you might do it (this is how I do this in some of my project management seminars):

Gather an appropriate group of experts. The trick with developing the group is to try to think of all areas of the project. For example, it might be appropriate to have someone from the quality department in the group. You might have someone from the training department if you have to conduct training to turn your product over to your customer. Try to cover as many bases as possible.

Once you have your group, give them all an ample supply of sticky notes. Then describe the project as best you can. It's okay to not be too specific but you want to maintain scope (and control of your audience). The less specific you are the more activities you'll get, although many may be out of scope. If you're too specific you'll miss activities, but there are plenty of opportunities to catch them later. You'll find the middle-ground without much difficulty.

Once you've described the project, let the members of the team individually write done EVERY activities they would consider for this project – one activity per sticky note. Make sure they write legibly. Put the results on a wall.

You'll end up with many activities. You'll have some duplicates, some high-level, some medium-level, some low-level activities. Now, with the group's help, sort out the activities into a hierarchy. Take the high-level activities and see if any of the medium or low-level activities help make it up. Then ask the team, "Are there any other low-level activities we need to do make sure we complete this high-level activities?" (remember: nothing missing). Then ask if there are any activities we really don't need to do to complete this high-level activity (remember: nothing extra).

You'll also find some low and medium-level activities with no higher-level activity. Go ahead and simply add them, continuing to facilitate as described above.

While this technique will not produce a thorough WBS, it is a great way to get started. Brainstorming is a creative exercise, not an analytical one. Therefore, there will be activities missing. That's okay; that's why we combine several techniques to produce a thorough WBS.

In addition to getting a WBS started it's a great team-building exercise and it's amazing the activities you didn't think of that your team did. Give it a try. I think you'll like it.

## Expert Analysis

Subject matter experts in all fields already know the list of activities they need to do to get something done. One technique I use to build my WBS's is simply ask an expert who has done it and have them do an analysis of the steps needed to complete their part of the project. To simplify it, tell them you simply need a checklist of all the steps. You'll get a reasonably good list. Scientists, marketers, engineers, accountants, and process engineers all know what they need to do to get something done.

The trick is that since this information is usually in their head, they tend to assume everyone else knows it, so they tend to leave things out. Ask an accountant how they develop annual financials and you'll hear things like: auditing, closing entries, adjusting entries, profit and loss. They'll give you a nice description of how that flows. At least in my experience they'll forget to tell you that you have to take inventory. "Well, everyone knows that, it's part of the adjusting entries!", they'll tell you.

Every expert in every discipline does it. I do it (even though I try not to). In order to become an expert, certain aspects of your job simply become intuitive.

I've found that challenging each analysis helps when building a WBS with subject matter experts. This doesn't mean I don't trust my experts. It's simply a tool to have them explain those intuitive actions they assume everyone knows.

How do you do this if you're not an expert? I just ask "stupid questions". As they're explaining it, I'll ask questions like, "where'd you get that from?", "why do you have to do that?", "were does that go?". Ask anything that comes to the top of your head. Some of these questions will annoy them. Prepare them in advance by describing what you're doing and why, and they'll get over it quite quickly. Some will actually challenge them, which isn't a bad thing. Either way, you get the results you want: a clean and thorough WBS.

## Templates

I have a philosophy that I find comes in handy:

**_It's easier to criticize something that exists than it is to create something from scratch._**

So, if you're stuck, go find a template. There are millions of them on the web. Some will cost money, most are free. They most certainly won't be perfect and probably won't even be that good, but they can be a start. They'll give you ideas and they'll offer you structures you haven't see before. Use your favorite search engine and poke around, you'll find something to get you started. I'll cover these in more detail later in this book.

You'll find a few on my web site at: AllyBusiness.com/dpw-simplified.

## Mind-Mapping

You already know that a WBS is a hierarchy: a decomposition of a large unit of work into smaller units of work. This is the way the mind works. The human mind likes hierarchies. Libraries have floors, floors have rooms, rooms have isles, isles have cabinets, cabinets have shelves, shelves have books and books have chapters… We just think this way.

A mind map is nothing more than a hierarchical decomposition of whatever you're thinking of. Every book I've written started out as a mind map. I brainstorm ideas, create the mind map, and organize the ideas into a logical flow and hierarchy. If you have mind mapping software, you may discover it already has the hooks and handles in it for WBS's. The practice of using mind mapping software to create WBS's is so prevalent that the software developers are starting to put scheduling and resource allocation features into their software. Also note that there's a lot of free mind-mapping software out there to help you get started.

The other advantage of mind mapping software packages is that collapsing and expanding the work elements is inherently easy. This not only eases creating the map, but also makes it easier to communicate the WBS to other stakeholders.

## Facilitated Session

Facilitated sessions are likely the most common method for WBS development, especially for larger projects. Here, a facilitator (usually the project manager) will gather a group of appropriate subject matter experts (SMEs) to create some part of the WBS. I almost always use this technique for creating the high-level elements of my WBS for larger and complex projects. There are several advantages to this technique:

- SMEs know what has to be done and how to do it.
- It starts building your team as they work together to create the WBS.
- The team buys-into the project as they're the ones creating it.
- The entire team learns what each of the other team members need to do their job.
- It's easy to delegate the more detailed aspects of the WBS during these sessions.

While these sessions can be run informally, I generally prefer a more formal method. To do this, I employ my earlier philosophy that criticizing something is easier than creating from scratch. Therefore, I create a high-level draft before the session to use as a template. THIS IS IMPORTANT: don't make the initial draft too good. If it's too good, the team will simply accept it as is and you'll be stuck with a bad plan. It's not unusual for me to put an obvious mistake in the first part of the WBS, hoping someone will catch it. As they find the error, they'll tend to look for more errors. This is exactly what I want. I want them to criticize it! I want them to challenge it. I want them to take ownership of it.

Here's exactly how I run this facilitation. First, come up with the highest level of the WBS. I usually use phases. I give each phase a title and a key objective. Don't be too fancy with this, it's designed to be criticized. Next, list the key deliverables you'll create in each phase. Next, list the high-level actions needed to create those deliverables. For more formal sessions I'll also identify a few risks associated with each phase. Figure 1 shows the format for my template. As you can see, it's not fancy. I don't want it to be.

*Figure 3  - Phase Development Worksheet*

**Ally Business Developers**
*Move Forward*    Phase Development Worksheet

Project: _____

**Phase ___ :** _____

Phase Goal:

Phase Deliverables:

Summary Level Tasks:

Risks:

© 1995 – 2014 Ally Strategic Partners, Inc. All rights reserved.

I create one sheet for each phase. Again, don't be too accurate or formal. I then take them to my local print shop and have them printed on large paper: typically about the size of a flip-chart sheet – 20"x30" works well. Most office service and supply houses will do this for you. Most independent printers also have sufficient equipment for this. If I have the budget, I have them laminated so I can write on them and erase, but lamination is not mandatory.

For the planning session take the sheets and tape them to a wall in the proper sequence. Tell the team you did this quickly, just to get started (which is the truth). Run through it and ask challenging questions. You already know my two favorites: anything missing, anything extra? Ask if there are any other deliverables we need to create in each phase. Challenge all aspects of the project. You can ask general questions like:

- Where should we build the test plans?
- Where should we start planning the turnover training?
- Where should we communicate with the clients and other stakeholders?
- When should we think about outsourcing?
- Do we need a separate integration (or whatever) phase?
- Where should we hold the design review?

For each key activity, find the appropriate subject matter expert and ask specific questions, like:

- If you start this activity here, will you have everything you need to do it right?
- Would it be better to move this task to another phase?
- How will you ensure the quality of that task?
- What should you do after you do this task?

The questions don't have to be fancy. Don't be afraid to ask "stupid" questions. They're the subject matter experts, you're not. But since they are, it's easy for them to assume things they shouldn't assume. That's the purpose of your questions: to find and challenge their assumptions. I have a philosophy:

**Assumptions make projects late!**

Frequently, you'll have someone say they're not sure about something. That's fine. We're at the early stages of planning; this is normal. But be careful, don't immediately assign the investigation to the one who discovered it. Find the appropriate SME to handle it. If you always assign it to the discoverer, everyone will stop discovering problems to keep their workload down.

As a final wrap-up, I ask for risks for each phase. I'll already have a few identified and pre-printed on the sheets, but I'll also solicit risks from the SMEs. Don't stop there! Frequently, you can reduce or even eliminate a risk by altering the WBS. Moving actives to earlier phases frequently reduces risks. Adding minor reviews or small additional cross-checking activities significantly reduces many risks. Now's the time to do this… at the beginning when it doesn't cost you anything.

When you're done, your once-pretty and likely expensive phase development worksheets should be a mess. They should have all kinds of markings, arrows, things written on the sides, cross-outs, etc. That's good! That's the sign of a well-rung-out plan! I like messy flip-charts!

Now, take the results and start building your formal WBS.

## Combining Techniques

None of the techniques I presented are mutually exclusive. Feel free to combine these techniques at appropriate places while planning. Here's a strategy to get you started:

1.  Run brainstorming session to get the basic tasks and activities.
2.  Use a mind-map to ring out the high-level flow using analysis. Engage your SME for this process.
3.  Take that, mess it up a bit, and run the facilitated session I mentioned above.
4.  Take the results of that and formalize the plan. Note that it's the SMEs that should do this step.

Do these steps and I promise a solid WBS. It may not be perfect the first time but will be really solid. Expect LOTS of tasks and activities. Also expect team buy-in!

Michael B Bender

# 4 SOLIDIFYING YOUR PLAN

Your WBS at this point is off to an excellent start. However, you're not quite done yet. In this chapter, we'll cover those areas frequently missing from WBS's. Remember, if it's not in the WBS we won't estimate it and our project will be late. First, we'll look at all those other activities you'll find in most projects. These include communication, quality, risk and procurement. Then, we'll find additional drivers: those project drivers that you won't find in the charter or requirements documents. Then we'll look at the depth of the WBS to determine how many layers down we should go. Finally, we'll look at those little details too many project managers leave out.

## Project Requirements

Certainly, product requirements will drive most of the WBS elements you'll need. However, projects can be complex things and just building the deliverables, sadly, is only part of the game. Here are a few more project considerations. You may recall a brief discussion of *project* requirements from chapter 2. We expand on this here.

**Communication** is also a critical part of your project. The role of communication is managing stakeholder expectations which requires some effort. This will include gathering information, formatting it, and preparing and presenting reports and presentations. I like to have a separate project management section of my WBS, part of which includes planned communication (monthly project reviews with senior executives and clients, weekly meetings with the team, etc.)

**Risk** planning and mitigation is another area to consider. Experienced project managers spend a substantial amount of time handling risks. Not only do you want to include the tasks associated with planning and managing risks, you'll also want to take steps to prevent major risks from occurring. These are called preventive plans and you'll need to include them in your WBS.

**Procurement** is another area to consider. If you need to outsource any of your work, you'll have to include steps like creating the Statement of Work (SOW), creating the vendor selection criteria, writing the Request for Proposal (RFP), and reviewing responses. You'll also need tasks for monitoring the vendor including periodic reviews and accepting their deliverables.

**Quality** is critical in all projects. You'll need to write test plans and procedures. Include tasks for actually testing the products. Also, until your team understands that they may not be perfect, include tasks to repair or revise items that may not pass testing the first time. It's amazing how many people build things and expect them to pass quality testing the first time. It just doesn't happen like that. We're humans and we're just not that perfect.

As you can see, projects can be complex things. Your project may not need a lot of activities in these areas but don't leave them out.

## Additional Drivers

If you followed the guidelines offered earlier, you've considered communication, procurement, quality and risk. You should have activities to create your monthly status report to senior management. You should have activities to conduct risk reviews on a regular basis. You should have tasks to develop your quality test plans and procedures. You should have tasks to fix and revise work after reviews. For procurements, you'll need activities to: write the solicitation, write the acceptance criteria, issue the solicitation, conduct the bidders conferences, review the proposals, conduct the negotiations, and write the final contract. After the vendor's on board, you'll need tasks to review the contractor's work, conduct their risk and quality audits, hold regular status meetings with the vendor, etc.

A few other considerations:

- If the project is high-visibility, stakeholders will constantly interrupt you wondering how things are going. You'll want extra activities to handle them.

- If the project is high-risk, you'll want extra activities to review risks, solve problems and conduct rework.

- If your client is a new client, they'll tend to micro-manage you, so you'll want additional communication tasks.

- If you have a lot of vendors and new vendors, you'll need extra tasks for coordinating and management.

- If you have a new team, you'll need more than the usual team-building activities.

- You may need training activities if you're dealing with a new technology.

I truly don't wish to scare you, but I'd rather you be prepared. Remember: leave nothing out!

### How Deep do we Go?

Novice and experienced project managers alike struggle with how deep to take the WBS. Certainly, you can decompose the WBS to minute detail resulting in micro-management. Also, just as certainly, you can leave your activities too large which can make them ambiguous.

There are two hard-and-fast rules that determine WBS depth. These are not necessarily measurable, so some experience will be required to get them right. After I present them, I'll offer some guidelines to help you through your first few WBS's. The rules are:

1. The task owner (performer) has to completely understand the work.

2. The project manager has to be able to monitor and control the work.

Both of these rules boil down to the capabilities of the task owner (performer). If they're very experienced, you don't have to break the WBS down very far (at least for their tasks). If they're relatively new, you have to develop a more detailed WBS. Some guidelines follow.

I use two basic guidelines to help me through this. Neither is a hard-and-fast rule, and I typically combine both in my projects. Before I go too far into this, it's important to understand that as you grow in both experience and training, this criteria will change. Formal projects employ a concept involving work packages. These have very specific characteristics, but they are also a more advanced topic. For the time being, my two basic guidelines will serve you well.

While these are in no particular order, the first one I'll present is the five-deep guideline. I don't like to decompose my WBS more than five layers. Again, this isn't a hard-and-fast rule, just a general guideline. So, in a typical project, I'll have:

1. Project

2. Phase

3. Deliverable

4. Component

5. Activity

It's okay to go to six layers on occasion, but I find five is a reasonable number for a typical small to medium-sized project. If I have to go to six layers frequently, or I have to go to seven layers, I'll take that section of the project and make it a sub-project, then assign it to a group leader, or young project manager to handle that for me. This eases my ability to manage the overall project.

The second rule is more well-known (it's actually in the PMI standard). It's called the *8-80 rule*. This rule basically says that an activity shouldn't be less than eight effort hours or more than 80 hours of duration. It's important to note the distinction between the effort and duration designations. The eight effort hours means that if a person was dedicated to the activity, without interruption, they would be done in one day. Of course, we are frequently interrupted in our work, so an 8-effort-hour task may take several days.

The second limiter is that it should be no longer than 80 duration hours. This is a stronger guideline and one I employ quite frequently, even on larger projects. This guideline assumes a "typical" task performer will do the work. The typical task performer will have a year or two of experience, doesn't have to be a super-star, but shouldn't be an underperformer either: they are an average performer and relatively reliable. Experience has taught me that this typical task performer can handle a 2-week duration activity pretty handily. They can stay focused on it even with some interruptions, manager their time efficiently, and accurately provide status when asked. For someone just out of school you'll want to think about breaking the WBS down further into activities of about 2-3 days until they get used to working in a corporate environment.

So far I've offered two rules and two guidelines to help you satisfy those rules. Here are a few other considerations regarding depth of the WBS:

Status meetings: Most project managers hold weekly project status meetings. These are great times to both start new activities and confirm completion of existing activities. I like to build my activities on weekly increments where possible.

Avoid 3 weeks: A 3-week long activity is just awkward. It's hard for people to estimate their time. Each week would be 33% completion and it's just difficult. If you have someone with experience and they can handle a larger task, I actually prefer to go to 4 weeks (one month).

Ability to estimate   Remember, the hard-and-fast rule says that the person doing the work understands the work. One test I use to evaluate this is to see if they can give me a reliable and accurate estimate for the work. If they can then they likely understand the work and can manage it. If not, then break it down further until they can.

## What to Include and not Include

I've said several times to include everything. I've also said that assumptions make projects late. However, I also don't want to micromanage the project. We need balance. The purpose of this section is to offer guidance for finding that balance.

When I first start my project I'm definitely a micro-manager. This is by design. It's to avoid assumptions. For example, after a person completes a task they have to unit test it. After that, the task must pass quality review. The review will likely reveal some items to fix. So the task owner has to repair them. If there were a large number of such items, we might have to conduct another review. When that's done we want to make sure we document the component as-built. Then we can submit the component for integration. The WBS for each task might be as follows:

1. Build and test component A
   1.1. Build component
   1.2. Unit test component
   1.3. Repair until working
   1.4. Conduct quality review
   1.5. Repair quality issues
   1.6. Conduct 2$^{nd}$ quality review (if necessary)
   1.7. Repair quality issues
   1.8. Update as-built documentation
   1.9. Update project actuals (time and cost)
   1.10. Submit for integration

This might seem like a bit of overkill, but I promise that unless your team is experienced, they won't think of all this when they estimate the task and your project will be late. Too many team members think they'll pass the unit tests and quality reviews the first time so their estimates are wrong. They forget they have to update documentation and capture their actual time and cost for the activities for the project.

However, once they understand, once this becomes routine, then you don't have to micro-manage any more. You can just have one activity called "Build and test component A" and be done!

My WBS' are much more detailed at the beginning than they are at the end. After I've trained my team, after they understand how we do things, then I can be less specific in my WBS and lighten up on my micro-management.

Also note that you don't necessarily have to put all this detail into the WBS. You can create a standard set of checklists and refer to them in the WBS. I generally find this approach a bit more palatable for my team. Remember, a checklist is a small WBS. Here's the checklist from the example above:

### *Component Activity Checklist*

- ☐ Build component
- ☐ Unit test component
- ☐ Repair until working
- ☐ Conduct quality review
- ☐ Repair quality issues
- ☐ Conduct 2nd quality review (if necessary)
- ☐ Repair quality issues
- ☐ Update as-built documentation
- ☐ Update project actuals (time and cost)
- ☐ Submit to integration

Keeping a set of such checklists makes a project manager's job much easier and cleans up the WBS considerably. Create such checklists for tasks you and your team perform on a regular basis. These might include: presentations to senior management, customer visits, client audits and reviews, risk reviews, etc.

## The Solid WBS

Developing a solid WBS might seem a bit overwhelming initially. Learning the skills takes a bit of practice. However once you get the hang of it, you'll discover that building them is both easy and beneficial. Select those techniques you find comfortable and logical at the beginning. The rest will follow nicely.

# 5 PRESENTING AND REUSING YOUR PLAN

The WBS has many uses beyond identifying all the work. It is an excellent communication tool for stakeholders. It's useful for negotiating for resources. It allows the project team to validate scope by ensuring there is sufficient work to complete each deliverable. Also, so we don't waste effort, save your WBS as a template for future projects.

As a communication tool, the project manager uses the WBS to justify resources, identify the skills needed for the project, and communicate overall direction to higher-level executives. As a negotiation tool, you can use the WBS to negotiate for specific resources, justify training programs, and justify outsourcing where WBS when appropriate. As a scope validation tool, the WBS is an excellent cross-check to ensure the project will create all the deliverables required for success. The sections below offer the two most common ways to present a WBS and briefly describes their use.

## Hierarchical Charts

Hierarchical charts are an excellent method for presenting a WBS. It's my favorite method for several reasons. For example, the observer can view the project at any level they wish. Senior executives can view it at the higher levels while the project team can view it at the lower levels. Clients can look at deliverables and functional managers can look at the activities involving their people. Historically, this was the most common method for presenting WBS's. PMs would draw them by hand or have the engineering drafting department draw them. Microsoft Project® won't produce a hierarchical diagram so outline format has become more prevalent. More recently, project managers discovered that they can create a hierarchical chart using mind-mapping software so hierarchical is becoming more common again. You can find several examples of mind-map WBS's on my web site at AllyBusiness.com.

The key advantage to hierarchical format is you can see the WBS in two dimensions. You can see it flow in time and you can also see the decomposition downward. This makes it easier for the PM and the team to visualize the project flow, move tasks to more appropriate phases, understand precedence (task sequencing), and resource loading for each phase.

Use the hierarchical chart when communicating with senior executives, clients, or other high-level stakeholders. Collapse the lower-levels of the WBS so they don't see it. If you're using project management software, try to avoid using the Gantt chart display as your audience will tend to focus on the length of the bars rather than the overall project structure. Display the entire project, not just a single phase or section. Try not to go more than three to four layers deep with higher-level managers. Details aren't important to them; the overall project flow is. The resulting diagram will by very shallow (vertically) and very long (horizontally). See figure 4.

*Figure 4: High-Level WBS Presentation*

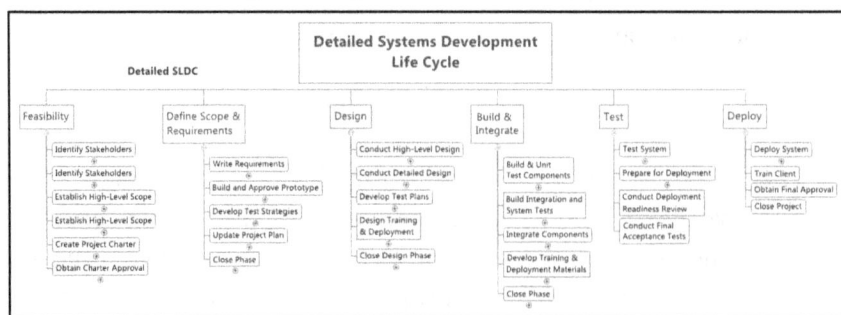

When communicating with your team, do exactly the opposite. Collapse almost all the elements of the WBS except your area of focus but display that area in appropriate detail. For example, if you're working on phase two, collapse all phases except phase two to hide their detail. Expand phase two to the greatest detail possible. See figure 5. You can expand the other areas of the project as needed.

*Figure 5: Detailed WBS Presentation*

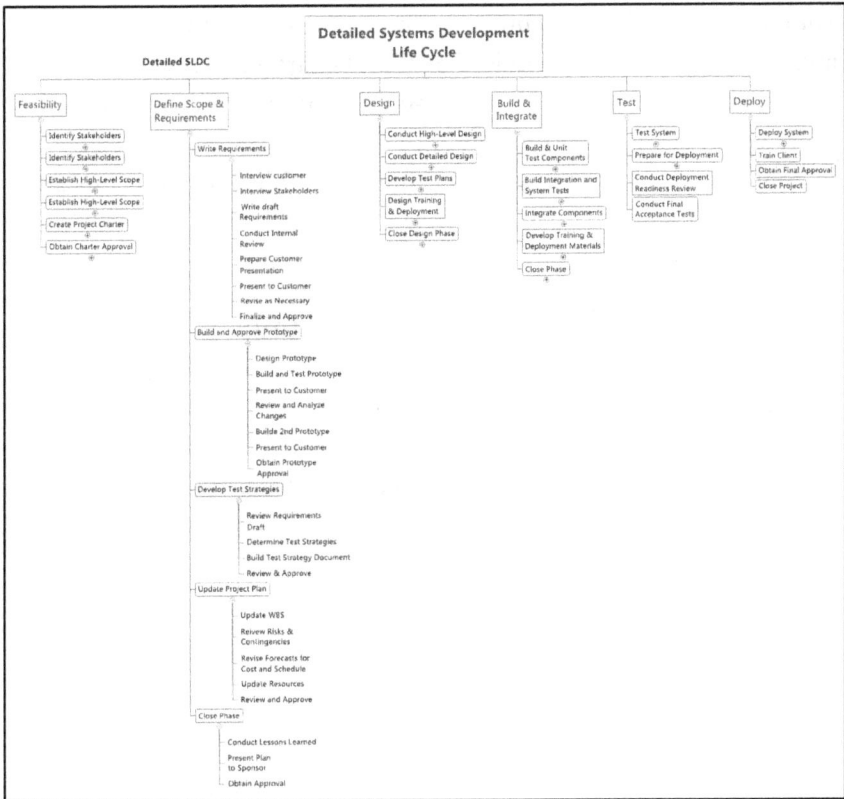

## Outline Format

The advantage of outline format is that you don't need any special software. Any word processor or spread-sheet program will produce an excellent result. Another advantage is that you can print it on standard paper. One disadvantage is that while you can still view the hierarchical relationships, it's more difficult to see the overall structure of the project. If you use project management software, you can expand and collapse the higher-level elements, but it still doesn't offer the structural perspective offered by the hierarchical format.

I use outline format when I need a paper version. I also use outline format when working with my team. I avoid outline when communicating with higher-level stakeholders for several reasons. Unless they understand the technology, it just looks like a bunch of words. The hierarchical relationships are difficult to understand in outline format. Also, executives are used to seeing Gantt charts so they invariably ask for the schedule. The Gantt chart is an excellent schedule communication tool, but a poor scope communication tool and an even worse negotiation tool.

Outline is useful for the team if the hierarchical relationships aren't important. They can focus on individual areas of the project easily, especially on a computer screen or handout.

## Negotiating with the WBS

The WBS serves nicely as a tool when negotiating for resources from senior management. Again, avoid using the Gantt chart as people will focus on the bars, not the project structure. It's easy for senior managers to see the need for resources when they focus on the structure.

## Validating Scope

As a scope validation tool, the WBS will ensure that your project includes all the tasks necessary to build all the deliverables promised to the customer. I continuously cross-check the WBS with customer deliverables to ensure completeness. Either hierarchical or outline will work for this. However, again, avoid the Gantt chart.

## Creating and Using Templates

One of the key characteristics of projects is that each project is somewhat unique. However, this doesn't mean there aren't similarities among projects. To the contrary, most projects exhibit a similar format and flow, especially within an organization. Every project requires the project manager to determine scope. This might involve writing requirements, building use-cases, demos, prototypes, JAD (*Joint Application Development*) sessions, or other methods. All project managers have to identify stakeholders. All project managers have to build products and verify quality. All project managers have to review risks, allocate resources, determine schedules, etc. No matter which methodology or life cycle you use, you still have to do these activities.

Within an organization it's not only common for projects to have a similar approach, it's advantageous. Once a group of stakeholders becomes familiar with the approach, once they understand the family of documents, once they see a WBS, they'll actually want to see similar patterns on the next project. The other reason it's advantageous to establish a common approach is that it eases your efforts, especially for the WBS. I highly recommend project managers create and continually update a WBS template for these reasons.

You can create a template from scratch or simply go back into your archives and find a similar project to use as a template. You will also find thousands of templates on the web. Poke around a bit and you'll find something that at least gets you started.

When you create and maintain your template, you'll want to capture some key information about tasks. The list below offers some insight into the kinds of information you'll want to maintain. You don't have to create all this information for every task at the beginning. Capture what you think will be useful then add more information as you use the template. In very short order you'll have a solid WBS template that produces excellent results. As your projects mature, you'll use this information more and more and later call it a *WBS Dictionary*.

Here's the list:

*Table 1: WBS Task Information*

| Task name | A descriptive name |
|---|---|
| WBS Code | Outline number that identifies the task |
| Purpose | Primary goal or purpose for this activity |
| Skills needed | Identify the kind of skills needed for the activity |
| Effort estimate | Rough estimate of the effort needed to do the work |
| Output | Product or deliverable the task produces |
| Risks | Risks associated with this activity |
| Success criteria | Key characteristics needed to deem the task complete and successful |

I offer one last comment regarding templates: include every task even if you need it infrequently. You'll discover that some tasks won't apply to every situation. Many people are tempted to delete these tasks from their template to clean it up. Don't. If you delete these tasks, you'll forget to include them later if you run across a project than needs them. Delete them when you create your actual WBS if you don't need them, but leave them in the template.

# 6 INTRODUCTION TO ADVANCED TOPICS

At this point you should have enough information to get started. Simple but rigorous project work planning produces excellent results so you should see an improvement in your projects quickly. You'll also begin to improve your skills just as quickly. So here's a brief introduction to some advanced topics. I'll cover these in more detail in the mid-level and high-level series of these books. In the meantime, these introductions should do you nicely. If you are truly new to WBS I do offer some caution. While I try to present these concepts as clearly and simply as possible, proper implementation takes a few years of practice. I suggest not trying to take them all on at once and don't fret over every detail. Take a lesson from the Japanese concept of *Kaisen*: get a little bit better each time.

## Defining the Layers

Hierarchical structures are not new to anyone. However, as you begin to rely on them and use them more extensively, you'll discover an advantage to specifically identifying the layers and assigning each layer special characteristics. For example, most project managers divide their projects into phases. In formal project management, phases must have very specific characteristics. Many project managers have a layer called *work packages*. Again, work packages have very specific characteristics. Other layers may include activities, tasks, deliverables, etc.

I briefly describe the more common layers below (phases, work packages, and activities). These are fairly common and consistently applied in project management. If your organization has already-established layers, please use those. If you and your organization are new to all this, then you might as well start off with the standard approach offered here.

## Phases

Most medium to large-scale projects are divided into phases. Phases are usually sequential and they usually represent a group of activities with a similar purpose or approach. For example, almost all development projects have a design phase. In this phase, we concentrate on all the activities needed to design the system. In this phase we may need to develop a prototype, figure out how to test the design when it's done, and establish throughput or other design characteristics; all these tasks are associated with designing the system. If you're remodeling a house almost all such projects will have a demolition phase where we rip out that part of the house we're working on, clean up the area, identify any hidden problems (hidden mold or discovering wires we didn't expect), and adjusting the plan. Again, these are all associated with the demolition.

If you decide to implement phases and want to start off on the right foot, one critical characteristic of phases is that they produce a major deliverable. The design phase will produce a design document. This phase will produce other deliverables as well but the primary deliverable is the design document. For the demolition phase, the key deliverable will be the "area ready to build", meaning the area is stripped of all useless material, cleaned and ready to go (yes, this is a deliverable).

For now, just make sure your phases end with a major deliverable. In more advanced texts, we'll use this to our advantage .

## Work Packages

Even advanced project managers misunderstand the advantages, characteristics, and importance of properly-defined work packages. Well-defined work packages are a blessing to every program and portfolio manager. They ease resource allocation; they allow portfolio and program managers to forecast resource levels months, even years in advance; they significantly improve outsourcing and vendor management; the list goes on. Certainly, I won't go into extreme detail regarding work packages in this book but I do want to start you off on the right foot.

For now, there are two key characteristics of work packages that aid the WBS. First, they produce a well-defined component of a deliverable. Continuing with our design phase example, the design of just the input module might be a work package. The design of the database module might be a work package. For our home remodel example, the actual demolition of one room might be one work package. The demolition of a second room might be another work package, cleanup of the two areas might be a third work package.

The second and perhaps more important characteristic of work packages is that the cost and schedule estimates are accurate.

For now, as you're developing your work breakdown structures, see if you can identify clear components that can be accurately estimated. Start identifying these as work packages. You'll find that delegating these is easier than other WBS elements.

## "Task" vs "Activity"

To my knowledge, the term "task" has no specific definition in the project management standards. The term "activity" is defined in the *PMBOK® guide* (PMI, 2013, p. 526) as, "A distinct, scheduled portion of work performed during the course of a project." Therefore, I personally use the term "task" to refer to any generic element of the WBS. I use the term "activity" to refer to a specific layer of the WBS that represents actual, assignable, and scheduled work. This is true for any style of WBS, deliverables-oriented or otherwise.

## Planning Packages

Projects exhibit a characteristic known as *progressive elaboration*. As the term suggests, we elaborate the project as we progress through it. In other words, as we work on the project, we understand more about it so our plan becomes more accurate and more detailed. This suggests something we already know, that at the beginning we can't know everything about this project.

Let's say we're running a 10-year project and we're in month number two. We know that some time out there in the future, maybe eight years from now, we'll have to integrate a lot of components to make a system. But we don't even have the system designed yet, so we can't know what we should integrate. This is where we use planning packages.

Think of a planning package as a place-holder. It's a task that's just not well defined yet. We know we have to do something but we're not quite sure how long it will take, what resources we'll need, or how much it will cost. We will eventually know these things but we don't right now.

Planning packages can be any size and shape. They can even represent entire deliverables or even phases. More commonly, they'll represent a group of work packages but even that's not a condition. Use planning packages as place holders. Give them the best estimates you can but acknowledging that these estimates are highly suspect. As you and your team progress through the project these planning packages will vanish, ultimately being replaced by well-defined phases, deliverables, work packages and activities. But for now, a place-holder will do fine.

## Work Package Dictionary

The PMI calls these WBS dictionaries. I call them work package dictionaries. Whichever term you select, the results are identical.

The *work package dictionary* (or WBS dictionary) is the list of all important information a project manager needs about each element in the WBS. As your WBS' become more sophisticated, you'll learn to capture resource requirements, success criteria, predecessors and successors, time and cost estimates, and many other pieces of information regarding each task. The collection of this information is called the WBS dictionary. We started to create one using Table 1 in the previous chapter.

On my web site (www.AllyBusiness.com), you'll find two versions of the forms I use: a simple version and a full version. Look under "PM Tools" and find the two Work Package Dictionary files. Pick the one you like. Tweak it, adjust it and make it useful for your company.

## Deliverables-Oriented WBS

Earlier, I mentioned the concept of the deliverables-oriented WBS. The most advanced WBS concepts to date take a deliverables focus. These are called deliverables-oriented WBS'. This is a major shift in the thought process for developing WBS', so I don't usually recommend it for novice project managers. Ironically, with this concept, the WBS doesn't contain any "work" at all. All the elements of the WBS consist of deliverables or components of deliverables. They are nouns not verbs, things not actions. So, in a design phase, a high-level element might be "design document" rather than "design the system". Note that the first example is a noun while the second example is a verb. In a deliverables-oriented WBS, a work package might be "input module design" rather than "design input module".

This distinction may seem trivial but as your projects and skills expand most project managers find substantial advantages to taking a deliverables approach rather than a work approach.

However, for smaller projects and newer project managers, the work approach is substantially better. Why? It's the western mind-set. We think in work, we don't think in "deliverables". When we wake up in the morning, we say to ourselves, "What do I have to do today?". We don't say, "What things do I have to create today?". When we delegate tasks to team members we say, "Go do this {task}"; we don't say, "Go build this {product}".

The other challenge is that many deliverables span multiple phases. It takes a bit of practice to learn how to divide a big deliverable up into smaller "sub-deliverables" that fit nicely into phases. It's substantially less difficult to divide work up into phases.

I recommend not taking a deliverables focus in the beginning. Even if you can handle it, it will likely confuse your team. As you and your team become more experienced and comfortable with WBS', start looking at them with a "deliverables" eye. That will make the transition smoother.

# 7 SUMMARY

In this text I presented the concept of the WBS in an easy-to-implement fashion. The Work Breakdown Structure is the core of project management. Proper application and development is critical to getting your project done on time and on budget. Fortunately, sophistication is not required until your projects become more complex and larger. For smaller and many medium-sized projects, a simple but accurate WBS will service you very nicely.

Get good at them. Practice them. When you find elements missing, go back to your WBS and put them in then save this version as your template for future projects. Above all else: don't leave anything out. Forget the sophistication if you have to. Forget defining the layers. Forget deliverables-oriented architectures. Forget the difference between activities and tasks. Just don't leave anything out. Start there. Develop the rest later. Remember from the first chapter:

**The purpose of the WBS is to define ALL the work required and ONLY the work required to make the project successful.**

As you practice and improve, then add sophistication as it presents itself. The WBS can be an easy item to get right, making it invaluable in project work.

**Good luck, and may all your projects be successful!**

# APPENDIX – LARGE FIGURES

Figures presented here are for illustrative purposes and are not necessarily designed to be thorough. You'll find the original mind maps on the web at <u>AllyBusiness.com/dpw-simplified</u>.

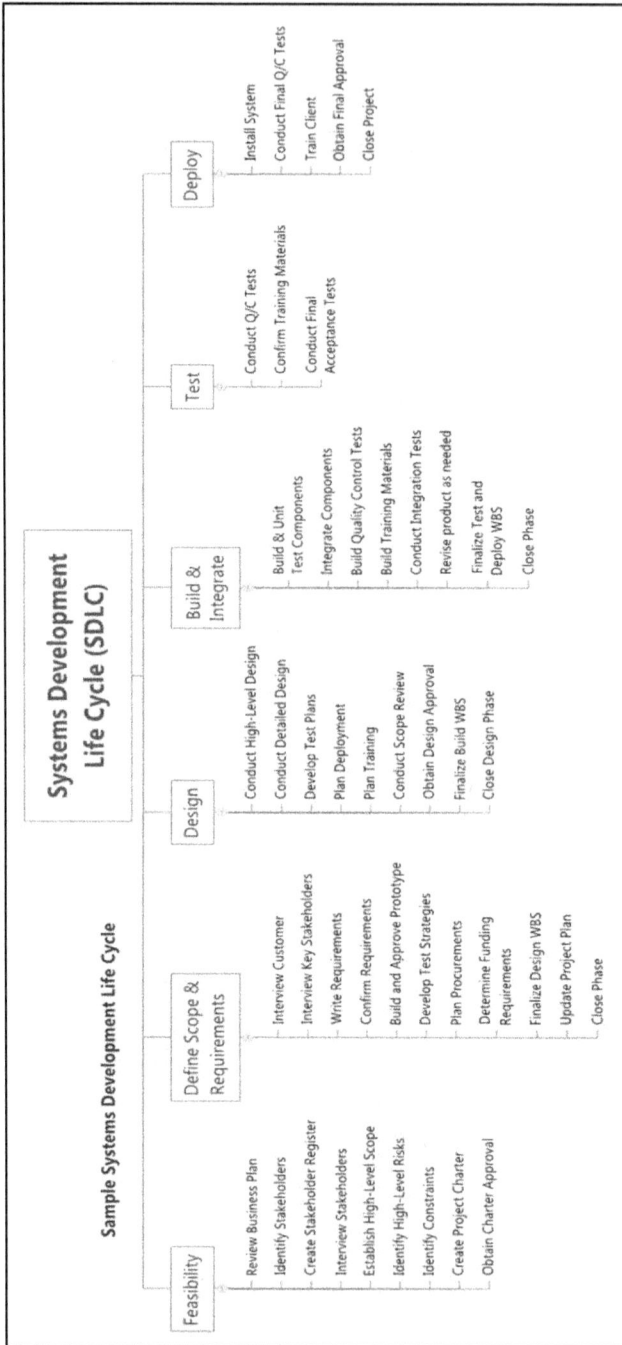

*Figure 6: Sample Systems Development Life Cycle*

Sample Systems Development Life Cycle

**Systems Development Life Cycle (SDLC)**

**Feasibility**
- Review Business Plan
- Identify Stakeholders
- Create Stakeholder Register
- Interview Stakeholders
- Establish High-Level Scope
- Identify High-Level Risks
- Identify Constraints
- Create Project Charter
- Obtain Charter Approval

**Define Scope & Requirements**
- Interview Customer
- Interview Key Stakeholders
- Write Requirements
- Confirm Requirements
- Build and Approve Prototype
- Develop Test Strategies
- Plan Procurements
- Determine Funding Requirements
- Finalize Design WBS
- Update Project Plan
- Close Phase

**Design**
- Conduct High-Level Design
- Conduct Detailed Design
- Develop Test Plans
- Plan Deployment
- Plan Training
- Conduct Scope Review
- Obtain Design Approval
- Finalize Build WBS
- Close Design Phase

**Build & Integrate**
- Build & Unit Test Components
- Integrate Components
- Build Quality Control Tests
- Build Training Materials
- Conduct Integration Tests
- Revise product as needed
- Finalize Test and Deploy WBS
- Close Phase

**Test**
- Conduct Q/C Tests
- Confirm Training Materials
- Conduct Final Acceptance Tests

**Deploy**
- Install System
- Conduct Final Q/C Tests
- Train Client
- Obtain Final Approval
- Close Project

*Figure 7: Detailed SDLC*

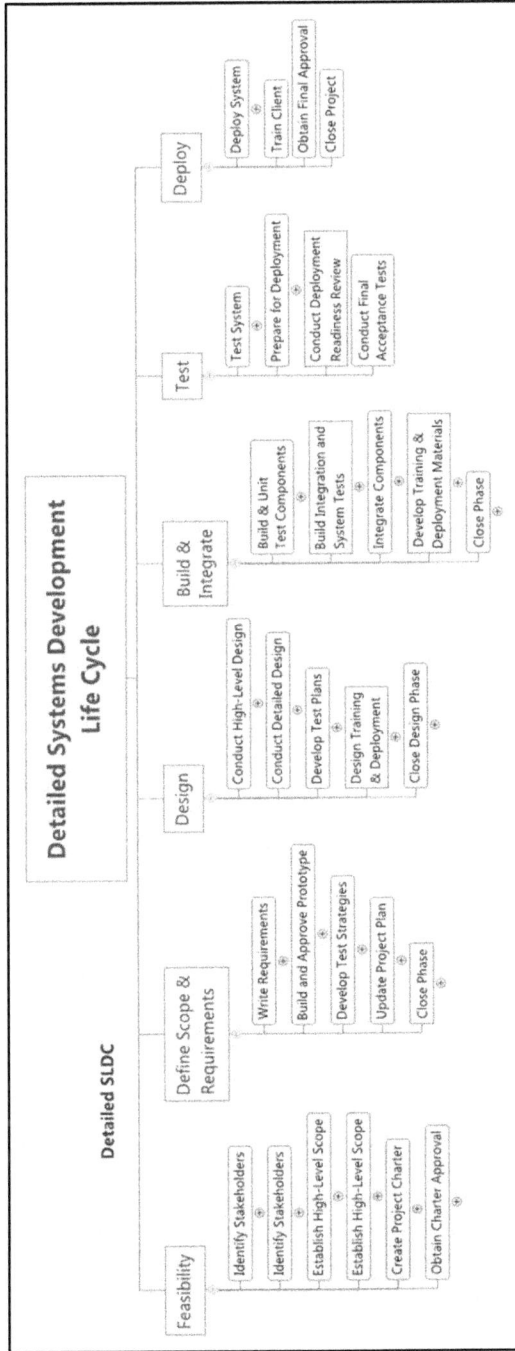

Detailed Systems Development Life Cycle

Detailed SLDC

**Feasibility**
- Identify Stakeholders
- Identify Stakeholders
- Establish High-Level Scope
- Establish High-Level Scope
- Create Project Charter
- Obtain Charter Approval

**Define Scope & Requirements**
- Write Requirements
- Build and Approve Prototype
- Develop Test Strategies
- Update Project Plan
- Close Phase

**Design**
- Conduct High-Level Design
- Conduct Detailed Design
- Develop Test Plans
- Design Training & Deployment
- Close Design Phase

**Build & Integrate**
- Build & Unit Test Components
- Build Integration and System Tests
- Integrate Components
- Develop Training & Deployment Materials
- Close Phase

**Test**
- Test System
- Prepare for Deployment
- Conduct Deployment Readiness Review
- Conduct Final Acceptance Tests

**Deploy**
- Deploy System
- Train Client
- Obtain Final Approval
- Close Project

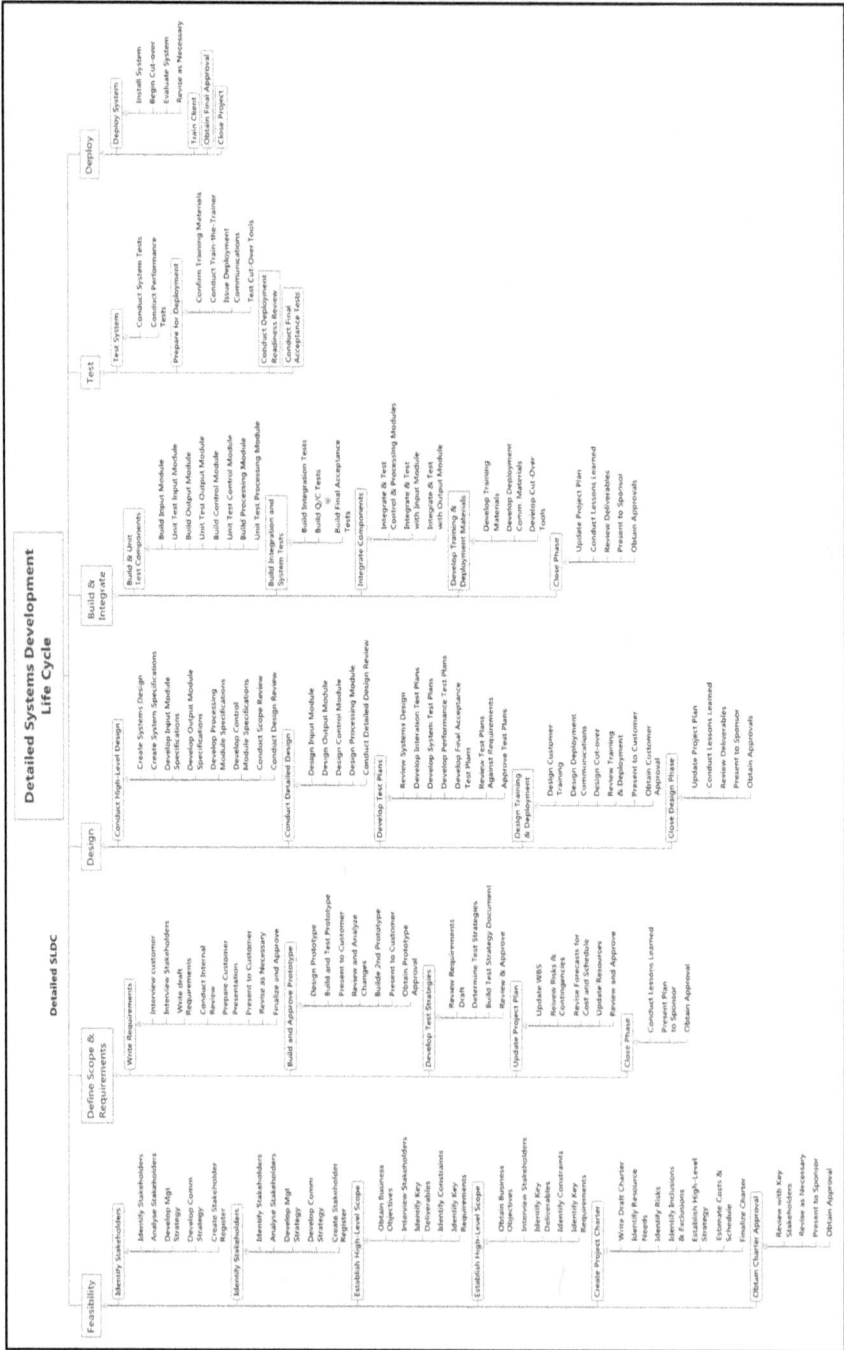

**Detailed Systems Development Life Cycle**

**Detailed SLDC**

### Feasibility

**Identify Stakeholders**
- Identify Stakeholders
- Analyze Stakeholders
- Develop Comm Strategy
- Develop Mgmt Strategy
- Create Stakeholder Register

**Identify Stakeholders**
- Identify Stakeholders
- Analyze Stakeholders
- Develop Mgmt Strategy
- Develop Comm Strategy
- Create Stakeholder Register

**Establish High-Level Scope**
- Obtain Business Objectives
- Interview Stakeholders
- Identify Deliverables
- Identify Constraints
- Identify Key Requirements

**Establish High-Level Scope**
- Obtain Business Objectives
- Interview Stakeholders
- Identify Key Deliverables
- Identify Constraints
- Identify Key Requirements

**Create Project Charter**
- Write Draft Charter
- Identify Resource
- Identify Risks
- Identify Exclusions & Exclusions
- Establish High-Level Strategy
- Estimate Costs & Schedule
- Finalize Charter

**Obtain Charter Approval**
- Review with Key Stakeholders
- Revise as Necessary
- Present to Sponsor
- Obtain Approval

### Define Scope & Requirements

**Write Requirements**
- Interview customer
- Interviews Stakeholders
- Write draft Requirements
- Conduct Internal Review
- Prepare Customer Presentation
- Present to Customer
- Revise as Necessary
- Finalize and Approve

**Build and Approve Prototype**
- Design Prototype
- Build and Test Prototype
- Present to Customer
- Review and Analyze Changes
- Builde 2nd Prototype
- Obtain Prototype Approval
- Present to Customer

**Develop Test Strategies**
- Review Requirements Draft
- Determine Test Strategies
- Build Test Strategy Document
- Review & Approve

**Update Project Plan**
- Update WBS
- Revise Risks & Contingencies
- Revise Forecasts for Cost and Schedule
- Update Resources
- Review and Approve

**Close Phase**
- Conduct Lessons Learned
- Present Plan to Sponsor
- Obtain Approval

### Design

**Conduct High-Level Design**
- Create Systems Design
- Create System Specifications
- Develop Input Module Specifications
- Develop Output Module Specifications
- Develop Processing Module Specifications
- Develop Control Module Specifications
- Conduct Scope Review
- Conduct Design Review

**Conduct Detailed Design**
- Design Input Module
- Design Output Module
- Design Control Module
- Design Processing Module
- Conduct Detailed Design Review

**Develop Test Plans**
- Review Systems Design
- Develop Integration Test Plans
- Develop System Test Plans
- Develop Performance Test Plans
- Develop Final Acceptance Test Plans
- Review Test Plans
- Approve Test Plans

**Design Training & Deployment**
- Design Customer Training
- Design Deployment Communications
- Design Cut-over
- Review Training & Deployment
- Present to Customer
- Obtain Customer Approval

**Close Design Phase**
- Update Project Plan
- Conduct Lessons Learned
- Review Deliverables
- Present to Sponsor
- Obtain Approvals

### Build & Integrate

**Build & Unit Test Components**
- Build Input Module
- Unit Test Input Module
- Build Output Module
- Unit Test Output Module
- Build Control Module
- Unit Test Control Module
- Build Processing Module
- Unit Test Processing Module

**Build Integration and System Tests**
- Build Integration Tests
- Build Q/C Tests
- Build Final Acceptance Tests

**Integrate Components**
- Integrate & Test Control & Processing Modules
- Integrate & Test with Input Module
- Integrate & Test with Output Module

**Develop Training & Deployment Materials**
- Develop Training Materials
- Develop Deployment Comm. Materials
- Develop Cut-Over Tools

**Close Phase**
- Update Project Plan
- Conduct Lessons Learned
- Review Deliverables
- Present to Sponsor
- Obtain Approvals

### Test

**Test System**
- Conduct System Tests
- Conduct Performance Tests

**Prepare for Deployment**
- Confirm Training Materials
- Conduct Train-the-Trainer
- Issue Deployment Communications
- Test Cut-Over Tools

**Conduct Deployment Readiness Review**
- Conduct Final Acceptance Tests

### Deploy

**Deploy System**
- Install System
- Begin Cut-over
- Evaluate System
- Revise as Necessary
- Train Client
- Obtain Final Approval
- Close Project

52

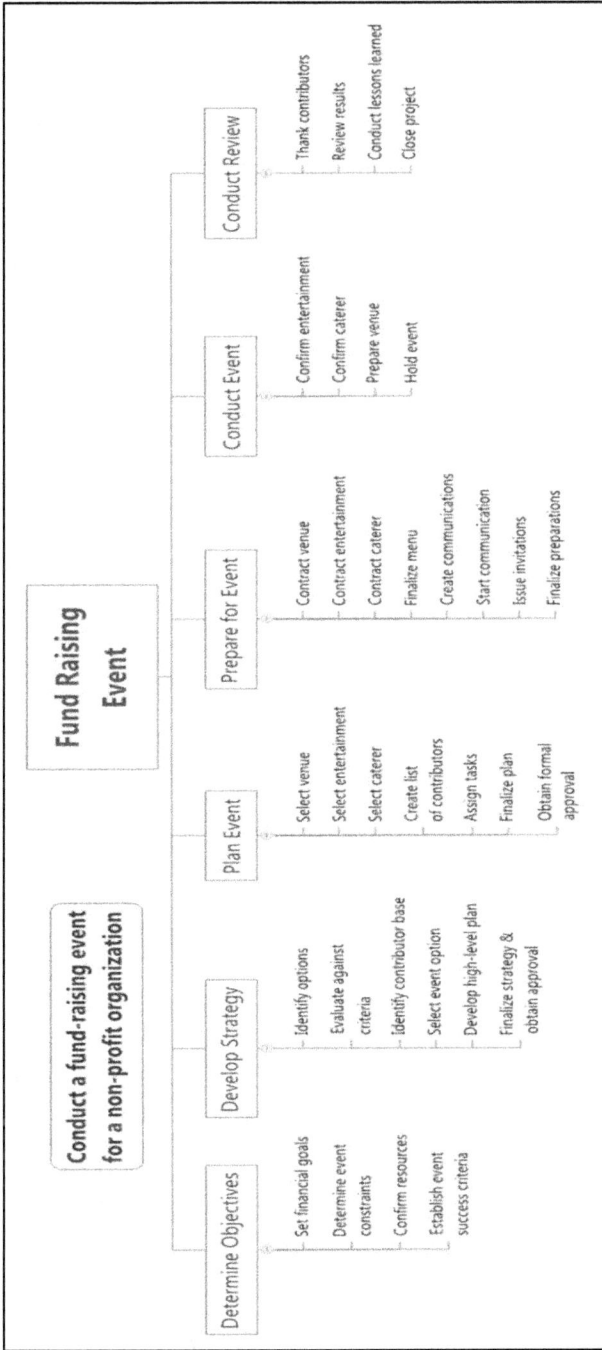

Figure 9: Sample WBS for Fund-Raising Event

# ABOUT THE AUTHOR

Mr. Bender, president of Ally Strategic Partners, Ltd., is an accomplished speaker, author and seminar leader in the business management field. Specializing in all areas of strategic planning, work flow management and resource management, Mr. Bender is a frequent speaker for: Rutgers University Business School, DeVry University – Becker Professional Education, Global Knowledge, American Management Association and many other companies, organizations and universities. Mr. Benders' keynote speeches specialize in advanced concepts in resource management across strategic plans, programs and portfolios for industry, non-profit, educational and government sectors.

Mr. Bender began his career in high-technology fields. Specializing in computer systems development, Mr. Bender worked both as a subject matter expert and project manager on such projects as: the Hubbell Space Telescope, the US weather radar system, air traffic control systems in three continents, satellite launches, cable television automation systems and many other technology-based projects. Through this experience, Mr. Bender developed his unique skills in advanced program management, resource allocation and strategic planning.

Mr. Benders' additional books in project management include:

- *Project Risk Management – Simplified!, The Project Management Mini-Series.* Ally Publishing Group, 2013

- *A Manager's Guide to Project Management*, Financial Times Press, 2010

- *Setting Goals and Expectations*, Virtual Bookworm Publishing, 2004

For more information about this or other books, visit Ally's web site at www.AllyBusiness.com.